Helen Steiner Rice's

Poems of Faith

Helen Steiner Rice's

Poems of Faith

LITTLEBROOK

LITTLEBROOK PUBLISHING, INC.
PRINCETON, NEW JERSEY 08540

Book design by Holly Johnson at the Angelica Design Group, Ltd.
Illustrations by Judith Fast

Unless otherwise noted, Scripture quotations in this book are from the King
James Version of the Bible

Library of Congress Cataloging in Publication Data

Rice, Helen Steiner.
    Helen Steiner Rice's Poems of faith.

    1. Christian poetry, American.   I. Title.
II. Title: Poems of faith.
PS3568.128P6   811.54   81-15596
ISBN 0-89952-086-3   AACR2

Contents

8 • *Poems of Prayerful Praise and Thanksgiving*

Introduction

The writing career of Helen Steiner Rice (1900-1981) began in earnest in 1931 when, following her husband's death, she joined Gibson Greeting Cards in Cincinnati, and it lasted for nearly five decades. During that time, she composed an unbelievable number of poems (she once estimated the total at over two million)—humorous poems, sympathy poems, birthday poems, Christmas poems, anniversary poems, wedding poems, get well poems, graduation poems, Mother's Day poems, Father's Day poems; few were religious or inspirational because, according to Mrs. Rice, first-rate greeting card companies frowned on cards bearing religious sentiments.

Until the 1950s, most of her "faith" poems were written for and sent to close friends as personal greetings on special occasions. Some of those messages eventually made it into print, however, and it was one of them, "The Priceless Gift of Christmas," read on the Lawrence Welk television show in 1960, that introduced the nation to Mrs. Rice and led to her recognition as "America's most popular inspirational poet."

From 1960 until her death, her writing focused primarily on inspirational messages about giving, faith, love, hope, kindness, steadfastness, honesty, sacrifice—virtues that reflected her deep Christian convictions and commitment. When this book was being planned, we asked Mrs. Rice to select her favorite "faith" poems, poems that glorified Christ and His love.

She had many suggestions, some that were well known, others that had not appeared in books before. Among her suggestions were that we include "When I Must Leave You" and "The End of the Road Is But a Bend in the Road," but the one she most wanted to appear in this book was "A Child's Faith." We were glad to comply, because each is heart-touching in its simplicity, each is beautiful in its clarity. That, in the last analysis, may have been Mrs. Rice's greatest gift as a writer, to cut through theological fogs and make deep spiritual truths church-bell clear.

And it is to her poems that make faith clearest that we have turned in this volume. Our hope and prayer is that Mrs. Rice's words serve to strengthen your faith and guide you whenever you read them.

—*The Editors*

A Memorial Tribute: She Was Different
by Fred Bauer

The message was one of the first things I saw upon returning home from an over-Easter trip to Florida: *Mrs. Rice died last night. Please call me. Mary Jo Eling.* (Mary Jo assisted Mrs. Rice with great devotion and talent for many years.)

The death of my friend Helen Steiner Rice did not take me by surprise. It had been expected. Yet, somehow, I was not prepared for it. Bigger-than-life people such as Helen seem so invulnerable, yet her passing drove home that old truth that there is absolute democracy in death; it plays no favorites, never discriminates.

When I had visited her in a Cincinnati convalescent home a month earlier, it was obvious that she was failing. She had lost much weight and her always-penetrating, always-flashing eyes were more weary than penetrating, more soft than flashing. Still, her hair—once a vibrant auburn, now subdued by gray—was neatly combed, upswept and stacked atop her head in the way she liked it and her face was brightened with make-up. ("Especially for your visit," a nurse whispered.)

When I arrived, she extended her hand for mine and drew me to her for a kiss. Tears formed in her eyes as she told me, "I'm so glad you came, Fred." Her voice like her body had grown small. Lost was the timbre and sharp inflection she used to punctuate her speech.

But our conversation was animated. We talked in spurts, recalling many shared memories. She wanted to tell me about some letters she had received, including one from President Carter in recognition of her eightieth birthday. And I wanted to share with her some of the warm responses that I had heard about her latest books. I also told her about the progress of this book.

We talked about the future, too. "I'm ready to go be with the Lord," she said with conviction. "I can't wait to shed this aching body."

"That may be, but the Lorain Tornado may have many miles to go yet," I replied. She smiled broadly at the mention of her nickname. As a young lady in her twenties, she had spoken all over the country, often on behalf of women and their potential in the business world. She was obviously a woman before her time. Once she was scheduled to speak at Cedar Point, a Lake Erie resort near her hometown of Lorain, Ohio, but a tornado canceled the date. "The real Lorain Tornado, Helen Steiner Rice, will be rescheduled," the local newspaper reported, and the nickname stuck.

"No, I have had enough of this life. I'm ready for heaven," she continued.

"What are you going to do in heaven?" I asked.

"Sit and rest." She laughed at the thought before adding, "and listen to the beautiful music."

"And write a few poems, I'll bet."

"Oh, yes, I'm sure I'll do some writing. I think we'll all have time to do the things we love."

But now late afternoon shadows were inching their way across the grounds outside, reminding me of my plane schedule. I rose to go, knowing in my heart that I would probably not see her again.

"I understand the flowers are beautiful here in the spring," I said.

"Yes, gorgeous," she answered.

"If I come back will you show them to me?" I was trying to find a positive exit note and she sensed it.

"Sure I'll show them to you. You can push me around the place in a wheelchair and I'll show you flowers like you've never seen."

We kissed again and I turned to go, but at the door I looked back and gave her a wink. "I love you, Helen," I whispered. She nodded, smiled brightly and blew a parting kiss.

Some day I must go back, some pretty spring day when the flowers are in bloom, and see the beauty she never got to show me.

It was the memory of my last meeting with Helen that was most vivid when I learned of her death, but it was only one of many that rushed to mind. To ponder them, I went to my study and closed the door. There, alone, I pulled a correspondence folder from my files and re-read some faded letters that we'd exchanged over the years. I also re-read some of her poems which brought to mind mutual writing projects we'd shared.

My first contact with her came when I wrote to her about a magazine article for *Guideposts*. Norman Vincent Peale and Leonard LeSourd had signed me on as an editor for the magazine not long before. "Everyone loves your poems," I had written, "but they want to know more about the woman behind them."

She wrote back that she was too busy to sit still for an interview. Furthermore, she said that she wasn't much interested in being written about. "I'm just another worker in the vineyard of the Lord, trying to do God's will. All I have to say is in the thoughts He places on my heart, thoughts I put to rhyme."

Being unaccustomed to such flat turn downs, I tried again, thinking that maybe she perceived me as some hotshot New York City writer. This time I suggested that I stop in for a chat the next time I visited my mother in Northwest Ohio. "I grew up there," I noted, hoping that she would be drawn to a fellow Buckeye. "I also went to college at Bowling Green, began my newspaper reporting in Ohio and was a member 'of your denomination.'" A little research revealed that Helen was a Methodist.

Alas, all my attempts to establish common ground with the nation's "inspirational poet laureate" failed. She turned me down again—kindly but firmly—and that was all she wrote, and all I wrote, for several years.

Finally, I did talk her into a visit—"You are very persistent, young man," she said. Later, when she knew me better, she changed it to "pushy." But she quickly tempered her remark by interjecting that she too had that quality sometimes when it was needed to get things done, and that she admired perseverence.

Whatever, we got on well and I got my *Guideposts* article, albeit five years late. It was well received, at least partially satisfying the public's curiosity in Mrs. Rice's personal life. Titled "The End of the Road Is But a Bend in the Road," it discussed three testing periods in her life—the unexpected death of her father when she was 18, the death of her banker-husband who took his own life following the collapse of the stock market in 1929 and the death of her much adored mother.

The article may have served to renew book publishers' interest in her autobiography, because the subject resurfaced only to be rejected again—emphatically—by Mrs. Rice. Though gentle and very generous with her time and money (she gave huge amounts of both to worthy causes), Helen could be stone-wall firm, even feisty when pressed.

She did relent eventually, however, agreeing to do "a selective autobiography that focuses on God's goodness not mine." I was asked to co-author it and, because she was now in declining health I agreed. The result was *In the Vineyard of the Lord*, through which I got to really know her as a friend and wonderful Christian. Suffice it to say that her head was on straight and she knew what was important in life and what was not.

All of these memories and more coursed through my mind that day when I went to my study after learning of her death. And though I was warmed by all those rich recollections, something was missing. I longed to express my respect, my admiration, my affection for her. Finally, I did what all writers do in such circumstances: I went to my typewriter.

I composed a poem for her, titling it "She Was Different," because she certainly was. When Gertrude, her sister, heard the poem, she asked me to read it at Helen's funeral, which I did at Christ United Methodist Church, Lorain, Ohio, April 28, 1981. My tribute goes like this:

She was different, she was special,
    unique in a thousand ways,
She was giving, she was loving,
    and we'll miss her all our days.

There are those who covet fame
    and court it like a beau,
There are those who covet wealth,
    kneeling in its glow,
But she was different…

There are some who strive for praise;
    they yearn for world applause,
There are some who chase sweet comfort
    as their one and only cause,
But she was different…

There are some who race for power,
    sure 'twill bring them joy,
Some who long for pleasure,
    seeing time an endless toy,
But she was different…

Her legacy was friendship,
    she was so giving of her time,
Her bequest was her faith in God,
    her children: her books of rhyme.

She knew sorrow in great measure,
 and was stung by illness, too,
But neither could defeat her,
 nothing her faith subdue.

And when she heard death coming,
 she didn't cower in fear,
Instead she called out boldly,
 "My Lord, I'm over here."

"I'm going home to be with mother,"
 she told me, her eyes aglow,
"I'll see my dad and husband,
 they're waiting there, I know."

Of course, the Lord will welcome her,
 with His angels magnifying
The beauty of that celestial place,
 devoid of pain and crying.

And so instead of mourning
 as we remember her this hour,
We really should be celebrating
 the blooming of a flower.

For heav'n will be much richer
 when she puts her pen to rhyme,
Describing golden avenues
 with lyricalness sublime.

But forgive us, Lord, for pining,
 for wishing she were here,
It's hard to give up someone
 we have come to love so dear.

Because you see—
She was different, she was special,
    unique in a thousand ways,
She was loving, she was giving,
    and we'll miss her,
        miss her,
        miss her, all our days.

1

Poems to Brighten Your Day

Day by day I realize more and more that nothing really matters in this world except love—the love we receive from others and the love that we give in return.

—HSR

A Recipe for Happiness

Happiness is something
    we create in our mind,
It's not something you search for
    and so seldom find—
It's just waking up
    and beginning the day
By counting our blessings
    and kneeling to pray—
It's giving up thoughts
    that breed discontent
And accepting what comes
    as a "gift heaven-sent"—
It's giving up wishing
    for things we have not
And making the best of
    whatever we've got—
It's knowing that life
    is determined for us,
And pursuing our tasks
    without fret or fuss—
For it's by completing
    what God gives us to do
That we find real contentment
    and happiness, too.

No One Lives by Bread Alone

He lived in a palace
     on a mountain of gold,
Surrounded by riches
     and wealth untold,
Priceless possessions
     and treasures of art,
But he died alone
     of a *"Hungry Heart."*
For man cannot live
     by bread alone,
No matter what
     he may have or own...
For though he reaches
     his earthly goal
He'll waste away
     with a "starving soul"!
But he who eats
     of *Holy Bread*
Will always find
     his spirit fed,
And even the poorest
     of men can afford
To feast at the table
     prepared by the Lord.

Love suffers long, and is kind,
Love envieth not,
Love vaunteth not itself,
is not puffed up,
doth not behave itself unseemly,
seeketh not her own,
is not easily provoked,
thinketh no evil.
rejoiceth not in iniquity,
but rejoiceth in truth,
beareth all things,
believeth all things,
hopeth all things,
endureth all things,
Love never fails.
                    —*I Corinthians 13:4-8*

God's Gift Divine

Love is enduring
And patient and kind,
It judges all things
With the heart not the mind,
And love can transform
The most commonplace
Into beauty and splendor
And sweetness and grace...
For love is unselfish,
Giving more than it takes,
And no matter what happens
Love never forsakes,
It's faithful and trusting
And always believing,
Guileless and honest
And never deceiving...
Yes, love is beyond
What man can define,
For love is immortal,
God's Gift is Divine!

High Ideals Are Like Stars

In this world of casual carelessness
    it's discouraging to try
To keep our morals and standards
    and our *Ideals High*...
We are ridiculed and laughed at
    by the smart sophisticate
Who proclaims in brittle banter
    that such things are out of date...
But no life is worth the living
    unless it's built on truth,
And we lay our life's foundation
    in the golden years of youth...
So allow no one to stop you
    or hinder you from laying
A firm and strong foundation
    made of Faith and Love and Praying...
Remember that *Ideals*
    are like *Stars Up in The Sky,*
You can never really reach them,
    hanging in heavens high...
But like the mighty mariner
    who sailed the storm-tossed sea,
And used the stars to chart his course
    with skill and certainty,
You too can chart your course in life
    with high ideals and love,
For high ideals are like the stars
    that light the sky above...
You cannot ever reach them,
    but lift your heart up high
And your *life* will be as *shining*
    as the *Stars Up In The Sky.*

Be Glad!

Be glad that you've had such a full, happy life,
Be glad for your joy as well as your strife,
Be glad that you've walked in sunshine and rain,
Be glad that you've felt both pleasure and pain,
Be glad that you've tasted the bitter and sweet,
Be glad that your life has been full and complete,
Be glad that you've walked with courage each day,
Be glad you've had strength for each step of the way,
Be glad for the comfort you've found in prayer,
But be gladdest of all for God's tender care.

We know life's never measured
by how many years we live,
But by the kindly things we do
and the happiness we give.

He Never Sends Winter
Without the Joy of Spring

Springtime is a season
    of HOPE, and, JOY and CHEER,
There's beauty all around
    to see, and touch and hear.
So, no matter how downhearted
    and discouraged we may be,
New hope is born when we behold
    leaves budding on a tree,
Or when we see a timid flower
    push through the frozen sod
And open wide in glad surprise
    its petaled eyes to God.
For this is just God saying—
    "Lift up your eyes to me,
And the bleakness of your spirit,
    like the budding springtime tree,
Will lose its wintry darkness
    and your heavy heart will sing"
For God never sends THE WINTER
    without the JOY OF SPRING.

Helen Steiner Rice once said that she got her flair for writing and clothes, especially hats (Mrs. Rice was famous for her many colorful and elaborate hats), from her mother who was a talented seamstress and designer. Before marriage, Mother Steiner (nee Anna Bieri) worked in a Cleveland sewing establishment that catered to the city's wealthier women. After she was married, she lavished her talent on her daughters, Helen and Gertrude, going to great lengths to see that they were attractively dressed. "Mother made me feel like the most special daughter in the world," Helen recalled. And her daughter's adoration of pretty, petite mother was restated again and again in poems she penned in praise of mothers.

A Mother's Love

A Mother's love is something
    that no one can explain,
It is made of deep devotion
    and of sacrifice and pain,
It is endless and unselfish
    and enduring come what may
For nothing can destroy it
    or take that love away…
It is patient and forgiving
    when all others are forsaking,
And it never fails or falters
    even though the heart is breaking…
It believes beyond believing
    when the world around condemns,
And it glows with all the beauty
    of the rarest, brightest gems…
It is far beyond defining,
    it defies all explanation,
and it stills remains a secret
    like the mysteries of creation…
A many-splendored miracle
    man cannot understand
And another wondrous evidence
    of God's tender guiding hand.

"He was the gentlest man I've ever known," Helen Steiner Rice said of her father. "He never raised his voice at me or spanked me. He had no need to, because I wanted to please him more than anything." John Steiner, farmer turned railroad engineer, was forever exasperating his wife by laying off work to go hunting and fishing. Often, he took his daughter Helen with him—doubly exasperating his wife. " You'll turn the girl into a tomboy," she scolded. "Nonsense," he answered.

"The legacy he gave me was a love for the outdoors and all of God's handiwork," Helen said. When her father died during the influenza epidemic of 1918, Helen's plans to go to Ohio State to study law (the rarity of a woman studying law was noted in the local paper) had to be changed. She took a job instead and as a result her life took a turn that eventually led to a writing career and a world-wide ministry.

Fathers Are Wonderful People

Fathers are wonderful people
    too little understood,
And we do not sing their praises
    as often as we should...
And Father struggles daily
    to live up to *"his image"*
As protector and provider
    and "hero of the scrimmage"...
And perhaps that is the reason
    we sometimes get the notion
That Fathers are not subject
    to the thing we call emotion,
But if you look inside Dad's heart,
    where no one else can see,
You'll find he's sentimental
    and as "soft" as he can be...
Fathers are just *wonderful*
    in a million different ways,
And they merit loving compliments
    and accolades of praise,
For the only reason Dad aspires
    to fortune and success
Is to make the family proud of him
    and to bring them happiness...
And like our *Our Heavenly Father*,
    he's a guardian and a guide,
Someone that we can count on
    to be *always on our side.*

Flowers Leave Their Fragrance on the Hand of the Giver

There's an old Chinese proverb
    that, if practiced each day,
Would change the whole world
    in a wonderful way—
Its truth is so simple,
    it's so easy to do,
And it works every time
    and successfully, too.
For you can't do a kindness
    without a reward,
Not in silver or gold
    but in joy from the Lord—
You can't light a candle
    to show others the way
Without feeling the warmth
    of that bright little ray,
And you can't pluck a rose,
    all fragrant with dew,
Without part of its fragrance
    remaining with you.

Brighten Up the Corner Where You Are

We cannot all be famous
     or be listed in "WHO's WHO."
But every person great or small
     has important work to do.
For seldom do we realize
     the importance of small deeds
Or to what degree of greatness
     unnoticed kindness leads.
For it's not the big celebrity
     in a world of fame and praise.
But it's doing unpretentiously
     in undistinguished ways
The work that God assigned to us,
     unimportant as it seems,
That makes our task outstanding
     and brings reality to dreams—
So do not sit and idly wish
     for wider, new dimensions
Where you can put in practice
     your many "GOOD INTENTIONS"—
But at the spot God placed you

begin at once to do
Little things to brighten up
    the lives surrounding you.
For if everybody brightened up
    the spot on which they're standing
By being more considerate
    and a little less demanding,
This dark old world would very soon
    eclipse the "Evening Star"
If everybody BRIGHTENED UP
    THE CORNER WHERE THEY ARE.

2

Poems for Those Who Grieve

God does not comfort us only to make us more comfortable. He comforts us so that we may also become comforters.

—HSR

A Gateway to Life

Death is a Gateway
    we all must pass through
To reach that Fair Land
    where the soul's born anew,
For man's born to die
    and his sojourn on earth
Is a short span of years
    beginning with birth...
And like pilgrims we wander
    until death takes our hand
And we start on our journey
    to God's Promised Land,
A place where we'll find
    no suffering nor tears,
Where Time is not counted
    by days, months or years...
And in this Fair City
    that God has prepared
Are unending joys
    to be happily shared
With all of our loved ones
    who patiently wait
On Death's Other Side
    to open "The Gate"!

That Souls May Grow

May you find comfort in the thought
     that sorrow, grief and woe
Are sent into our lives sometimes
     to help our souls to grow…

For through the depths of sorrow
     comes understanding love,
And peace and truth and comfort
     sent from God above.

Sweet Recompense

After the clouds the sunshine,
 After the winter the spring,
After the shower the rainbow,
 For life is a changeable thing.

After the night the morning,
 Bidding all darkness cease,
After life's cares and sorrows,
 The comfort and sweetness of peace.

Because Christ Lives

A troubled world can find
Blessed reassurance
And enduring peace of mind…
For though we grow discouraged
In this world we're living in,
There is comfort just in knowing
God has triumphed over sin…
For our Saviour's Resurrection
Was God's way of telling men
That in Christ we are eternal
And in Him we live again…
And to know life is unending
And God's love is unending, too,
Makes our daily tasks and burdens
So much easier to do…
For the blessed Easter Story
Of Christ the living Lord,
Makes our earthly sorrow nothing
When compared with this reward.

He Cares

What more can we ask of the Saviour
    than to know we are never alone—
That His mercy and love are unfailing
    and He makes all our problems His own.

Tribute to a Friend

He will live in the hearts of the friends he made
    and be known always for the foundation he laid,
Because Goodness and Fairness never die—
    they go shining on like sun in the sky,
Just as Honor and Truth endure forever,
Death is powerless to destroy or to sever...
So his gallant soul has taken flight
    into a land where there is no night,
He is not dead, he has only gone on
    to a brighter, more wonderful dawn.

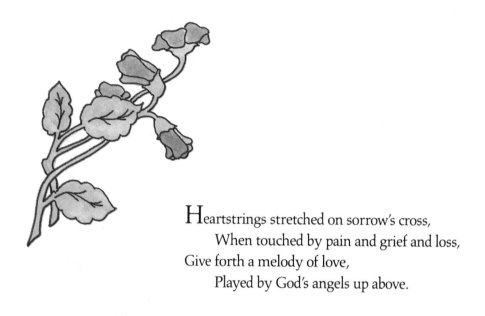

Heartstrings stretched on sorrow's cross,
    When touched by pain and grief and loss,
Give forth a melody of love,
    Played by God's angels up above.

More of Thee, Less of Me

Take me and break me and make me, dear God,
Just what you want me to be—
Give me the strength to accept what you send
And eyes with the vision to see
All the small arrogant ways that I have
And the vain little things that I do,
Make me aware that I'm often concerned
More with MYSELF than with YOU.
Uncover before me my weakness and greed
And help me to search deep inside
So I may discover how easy it is
To be selfishly lost in my pride—
And then in Thy goodness and mercy
Look down on this weak, erring one
And tell me that I am forgiven
For all I've so willfully done.
And teach me to humbly start following
The path that the dear Saviour trod
So I'll find at the end of life's journey
A HOME IN THE CITY OF GOD.

In All Things Give Thanks

Blessings come in many guises
  That God alone in love devises,
And sickness which we dread so much
  Can bring a very "healing touch"—
For often on the "wings of pain"
  The peace we sought before in vain
Will come to us with "sweet surprise"
  For God is merciful and wise—
And through long hours of tribulation
  God gives us time for meditation,
And no sickness can be counted loss
  That teaches us to "bear our cross."

44

He Will Take Me Safely Back

If Death should beckon me with outstretched hand
And whisper softly of "An Unknown Land,"
I shall not be afraid to go,
For though the path I do not know,
I take Death's Hand without a fear,
For He who safely brought me here
Will also take me safely back,
And though in many things I lack,
He will not let me go alone
Into the "Valley That's Unknown"...
So I reach out and take Death's Hand
And journey to the "Promised Land!"

The Promise of Eternity

All who believe in God's mercy and grace
  will meet their loved ones face to face,
Where time is endless and joy unbroken,
  and only the words of God's love are spoken.

Love Always Remembers

May tender memories soften your grief,
May fond recollection bring you relief,
And may you find comfort and peace in the thought
Of the joy that knowing your loved one brought—
For time and space can never divide
Or keep your loved one from your side
When memory paints in colors true
The happy hours that belonged to you.

When her mother, Anna Bieri Steiner, died February 20, 1945 in Lorain, Ohio, at the age of 73, Helen Steiner Rice composed a poem that reflected her mother's unshakeable faith in God. "I simply restated in verse her philosophy about life and death," Helen explained. Because the poem was so touching, many friends asked for copies. Then, friends of friends. When it was published on greeting cards, "When I Must Leave You" became an all-time favorite, having now been reprinted in the millions. Few poems by Mrs. Rice have drawn so much mail.

"Words cannot tell you what your poem, "When I Must Leave You," has meant to a dear friend of mine," one woman wrote. "She lost a 15-year-old son in a drowning accident. For a long time she was inconsolable. Then I gave her your poem. It has meant more than any other single thing."

When I Must Leave You

When I must leave you
    for a little while,
Please do not grieve
    and shed wild tears
And hug your sorrow
    to you through the years,
But start out bravely
    with a gallant smile;
And for my sake
    and in my name
Live on and do
    all things the same,
Feed not your loneliness
    on empty days
But fill each waking hour
    in useful ways,
Reach out your hand
    in comfort and in cheer
And I in turn will comfort you
    and hold you near;
And never, never
    be afraid to die,
For I am waiting
    for you in the sky!

God's Love Endures Forever

God's love endureth forever—
    what a wonderful thing to know,
When the tides of life run against you
    and your spirit is downcast and low,
God's kindness is ever around you,
    always ready to freely impart
Strength to your faltering spirit,
    cheer to your lonely heart.

God's presence is ever beside you,
    as near as the reach of your hand,
You have but to tell Him your troubles,
    there is nothing He won't understand,
And knowing God's love is unfailing,
    and His mercy unending and great,
You have but to trust in His promise—
    God comes not too soon or too late.

So wait with a heart that is patient
    for the goodness of God to prevail,
For never do prayers go unanswered,
    and His mercy and love never fail.

3

Poems of Peace and Reassurance

God never said die not, sorrow not, or suffer not, but He did say, 'Fear not!' And when you take the fear out of life, then all the terrible experiences—all the trials and all the suffering—become bearable.

—HSR

Give, and it will be given to you; good measure, pressed down, shaken together, running over, will be put into your lap. For the measure you give will be the measure you get back.

—*Luke 6:38 (RSV)*

Heart Gifts

It's not the things that can be bought
     that are life's richest treasure,
It's just the little "heart gifts"
     that money cannot measure...
A cheerful smile, a friendly word,
     a sympathetic nod
Are priceless little treasures
     from the storehouse of our God...
They are the things that can't be bought
     with silver or with gold,
For thoughtfulness and kindness
     and love are never sold...
They are the priceless things in life
     for which no one can pay,
And the giver finds rich recompense
     in GIVING THEM AWAY.

Not by Chance or Happenstance

Into our lives come many things
    to break the dull routine
The things we had not planned on
    that happen unforeseen,
The unexpected little joys
    that are scattered on our way,
Success we did not count on
    or a rare, fulfilling day—
A catchy, lilting melody
    that makes us want to dance,
A nameless exaltation
    of enchantment and romance—
An unsought word of kindness,
    a compliment or two
That sets the eyes to gleaming
    like crystal drops of dew—
The unplanned sudden meeting
    that comes with sweet surprise
And lights the heart with happiness
    like a rainbow in the skies...
Now some folks call it fickle fate
    and some folks call it chance,
While others just accept it
    as pleasant happenstance—
But no matter what you call it
    it didn't come without design,
For all our lives are fashioned
    by the HAND THAT IS DIVINE—
And every happy happening
    and every lucky break
Are little gifts from God above
    that are ours to freely take.

Teach Us to Love

God of love—Forgive! Forgive!
Teach us how to truly live,
Ask us not our race or creed,
Just take us in our hour of need,
And let us know You love us, too,
And that we are a part of You,
And someday may man realize
That all the earth, the seas and skies
Belong to God who made us all,
The rich, the poor, the great, the small,
And in the Father's Holy Sight
No man is yellow, black or white,
And peace on earth cannot be found
Until we meet on common ground
And every man becomes a brother
Who worships God and loves each other.

Precious Little Memories

Precious little memories
    of little things we've done,
Make the very darkest day
    a bright and happy one,

Tender little memories
    of some word or deed,
Give us strength and courage
    when we are in need,

Blessed little memories
    help us bear the cross
And soften all the bitterness
    of failure and of loss,

Priceless little memories
    are treasures without price,
And through the gateway of the heart
    they lead to paradise.

Lord, Calm Me Down Even When...

I know the hours are passing by
    and it's impossible to do,
All the things I planned on,
    but cannot carry through.

Mrs. Rice married a wealthy Dayton, Ohio, banker in 1929, but their marriage ended in tragedy. Distraught by losses that resulted from the stock market collapse, her husband took his own life. In 1931, Mrs. Rice joined Gibson Greeting Cards in Cincinnati. A short time later, she was named editor of the company's card line and for the next 50 years she wrote literally millions of verses for greeting cards. She was also a great motivator of the company's sales force. When speaking to the salesmen, she told them a legend entitled, "The Windows of Gold." It was so well received that she later put the little story into verse.

The Windows of Gold

There is a legend that has often been told
    Of the boy who searched for the Windows of Gold.
The beautiful windows he saw far away
    When he looked in the valley at sunrise each day.
And he yearned to go down to the valley below
    But lived on a mountain that was covered with snow,
And he knew it would be a difficult trek,
    But that was a journey he wanted to make.
So he planned by day and he dreamed by night
    Of how he could reach The Great Shining Light.
And one golden morning when dawn broke through
    And the valley sparkled with diamonds of dew
He started to climb down the mountainside
    with the Windows of Gold as his goal and his guide.
He traveled all day and, weary and worn,
    With bleeding feet and clothes that were torn,
He entered the peaceful valley town
    Just as the Golden Sun went down.
But he seemed to have lost his "Guiding Light,"
    The windows were dark that had once been bright.

And hungry and tired and lonely and cold
      He cried, "Won't You Show Me The Windows of Gold?"
And a kind hand touched him and said, "Behold!
      High On The Mountain Are The Windows of Gold."
For the sun going down in a great golden ball
      Had burnished the windows of his cabin so small,
And the Kingdom of God with its Great Shining Light,
      Like the Golden Windows that shone so bright
Is not a far distant place, somewhere,
      It's as close to you as a silent prayer,
And your search for God will end and begin
      When you look for Him and find Him within.

He Loves You—and Always Will

Someone cares and always will,
The world forgets but God loves you still,
You cannot go beyond His Love
No matter what you're guilty of—
For God forgives until the end,
He is your faithful, loyal friend,
And though you try to hide your face
There is no shelter any place
That can escape His watchful eye,
For on the earth and in the sky
He's ever present and always there
To take you in His tender care
And bind the wounds and mend the breaks
When all the world around forsakes
Someone cares and loves you still
And God is the Someone who always will.

On the Wings of Prayer

Just close your eyes
    and open your heart
And feel your worries
    and cares depart,
Just yield yourself
    to the Father above
And let Him hold you
    secure in His love.
For life on earth
    grows more involved
With endless problems
    that can't be solved—
But God only asks us
    to do our best,
Then He will "take over"
    and finish the rest.
So when you are tired,
    discouraged and blue,
There's always one door
    that is open to you—

And that is the door
    to the house of prayer
And you'll find God waiting
    to meet you there
And the house of prayer
    is no farther away
Than the quiet spot
    where you kneel and pray—
For the heart is a temple
    when God is there
As we place ourselves
    in His loving care,
And He hears every prayer
    and answers each one
When we pray in His name
    "THY WILL BE DONE"
And the burdens that seemed
    too heavy to bear
Are lifted away
    on the wings of prayer.

As Sure As Dawn Follows Darkness

If I can endure for this minute
Whatever is happening to me,
No matter how heavy my heart is
Or how "dark" the moment may be—
If I can but keep on believing
What I know in my heart to be true,
That "darkness will fade with the morning"
And that this will pass away, too—
Then nothing can ever disturb me
Or fill me with uncertain fear
For as sure as night brings the dawning
"MY MORNING" is bound to appear.

4

Poems to Strengthen Your Faith

I have no formula but faith, no Gospel but God, no creed but Christ and no love but the Lord. There can be no joy without Jesus.

—HSR

God Knows the Score

Have you ever been caught
    in a web you didn't weave,
Involved in conditions
    that are hard to believe?
Have you felt you must speak
    and explain and deny
A story that's groundless
    or a small, whispered lie?
Have you ever heard rumors
    you would like to refute
Or some telltale gossip
    you would like to dispute?
Well, don't be upset
    for God knows the score
And with God as your judge
    you need worry no more,
For men may misjudge you
    but God's verdict is fair
For He looks deep inside
    and He is clearly aware
Of every small detail
    in your pattern of living
And always He's lenient
    and fair and forgiving.

Cling to Your Standards

Cling to your standards
and "fight the good fight,"
Take a firm stand
for things that are right,
And let nothing sway you
or turn you away
From God's *old* commandments—
they are still *new* today.

God Bless America

America the beautiful
May it always stay that way—
But to keep "Old Glory" flying
There's a price that we must pay...
For everything worth having
Demands work and sacrifice,
And freedom is a gift from God
That commands the highest price...
For all our wealth and progress
Are as worthless as can be
Without the faith that made us great
And kept our country free...

Nor can our nation hope to live
Unto itself alone,
For the problems of our neighbors
Must today become our own...
So in these times of crisis
Let us offer no resistance
In giving help to those who need
Our strength and our assistance—
And the stars and stripes forever
Will remain a symbol of
A rich and mighty nation
Built on faith and truth and love.

A Prayer for Strength

O Lord, don't let me falter,
    don't let me lose my way,
Don't let me cease to carry
    my burden day by day...

O Lord, don't let me stumble,
    don't let me fall and quit,
O Lord, please help me find my "job"
    and help me shoulder it.

The Tree of Love

When we cut ourselves away
      from guidance that's divine,
Our lives will be as fruitless
      as the branch without the vine
For as the flowering branches
      depend upon the tree
To nourish and fulfill them
      till they reach futurity,
We too must be dependent
      on our Father up above,
For we are but the branches
      and He's The Tree of Love.

The Candle of Faith

In this sick world of hatred
And violence and sin,
Where men renounce morals
And reject discipline,
We stumble in "darkness"
Groping vainly for "light"
To distinguish the difference
Between wrong and right.
But dawn cannot follow
This night of despair
Unless faith lights a candle
In all hearts everywhere
And warmed by the glow
Our hate melts away
And love lights the path
To a peaceful, new day.

Jesus spoke again unto them, saying, I am the light of the world: he that followeth me shall not walk in darkness, but shall have the light of life.

—*John 8:12*

Bars and chains are not
the only things that enslave us,
We all make prisons of our own
from which only God can save us.

Prayers Are the Stairs
that Lead to God

Prayers are the stairs
We must climb every day,
If we would reach God
There is no other way.
For we learn to know God
When we meet Him in prayer
And ask Him to lighten
Our burden of care—
So start in the morning
And, though the way's steep,
Climb ever upward
'Til your eyes close in sleep—
For prayers are the stairs
That lead to the Lord,
And to meet Him in prayer
Is the climber's reward.

The Legend of the Wingless Birds

"Oh for the wings of a bird," we cry
        to carry us off to an untroubled sky,
Where we can dwell untouched by care,
        and always be free as a bird in the air...
But there is a legend that's very old,
        not often heard and seldom told,
That once all birds were wingless, too,
        unable to soar through the skies of blue—

For while their plumage was beautifully bright
        and their chirping songs were liltingly light,
They, too, were powerless to fly
        until one day when the Lord came by,
And laid at the feet of the singing birds
        gossamer wings as He spoke these words,
"Come take these burdens so heavy now,
        but if you bear them you'll learn somehow
That as you wear them they'll grow light
        and soon you can lift yourself in flight."

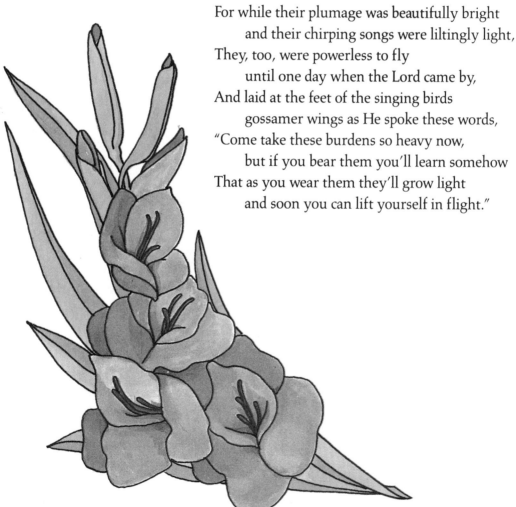

So folding the wings beneath their hearts,
    and after endless failures and starts,
They lifted themselves and found with delight
    the wings that were heavy had grown so light,
So let us, too, listen to God's wise words,
    for we are much like the wingless birds,
And if we would shoulder our daily trials
    and learn to wear them with sunny smiles
We'd find they were wings that God had sent
    to lift us above our heart's discontent—

For the wings that lift us out of despair
    are made by God from the weight of care,
So whenever you cry for the wings of a bird,
    remember this little legend that you've heard,
And let God give you a heart that sings
    as He turns your burdens to silver wings.

In 1960, Helen Steiner Rice received national attention when her beautiful poem, "The Priceless Gift of Christmas," was featured on the Lawrence Welk television show. Read by a performer named Aladdin, who had received it on a Christmas card sent by his sister in New York, the verse prompted thousands of letters requesting copies. Several other poems written by Mrs. Rice—"Praying Hands," "Prayer for Peace," a Mother's Day tribute to Astronaut John Glenn's mother and a memorial poem for President Kennedy—were all featured on the Welk program, but none generated the tremendous response as "The Priceless Gift of Christmas."

The Priceless Gift of Christmas

Now Christmas is a season
    for joy and merrymaking,
A time for gifts and presents,
    for giving and for taking...
A festive, friendly happy time
    when everyone is gay—
But have we ever really felt
    the *greatness of the day*...
For through the centuries the world
    has wandered far away
From the beauty and the meaning
    of the *Holy Christmas Day*...
For Christmas is a heavenly gift
    that only God can give,
It's ours just for the asking,
    for as long as we shall live...
It can't be bought or bartered,
    it can't be won or sold,
It doesn't cost a penny
    and it's worth far more than gold.

It isn't bright and gleaming
    for eager eyes to see,
It can't be wrapped in tinsel
    or placed beneath a tree...
It isn't soft and shimmering
    for reaching hands to touch,
Or some expensive luxury
    you've wanted very much...
For the *priceless Gift of Christmas*
    is meant just for the heart
And we receive it only
    when we become a part
Of the kingdom and the glory
    which is ours to freely take,
For God sent the Holy Christ Child
    at Christmas for our sake,
So man might come to know *Him*
    and feel *His Presence* near
And see the many miracles
    performed while *He* was here...
And this *priceless Gift of Christmas*
    is within the reach of all,
The rich, the poor, the young and old
    the greatest and the small...
So take *His Priceless Gift of Love,*
    reach out and you receive,
And the only payment that God asks
    is just that *you believe.*

The Answer Is Found in Doing Three Things

What must I do
     to insure peace of mind?
Is the answer I'm seeking,
     too hard to find?
How can I know
     what God wants me to be?
How can I tell
     what's expected of me?
Where can I go
     for guidance and aid
To help me correct
     the errors I've made?
The answer is found
     in doing three things
And great is the gladness
     that doing them brings—
Do justice—love kindness—
     walk humbly with God.
For with these three things
     as your "rule and your rod"
All things worth having
     are yours to achieve
If you follow God's words
     and have FAITH to BELIEVE.

One of Mrs. Rice's favorite "faith" poems was "A Child's Faith," which she wanted included in this volume. "When I was a child I attended Sunday School and sang 'Jesus Loves Me,'" she recalled. "I believed the words then, and I believe them now. It requires a childlike faith to really know the fullness of God's love."

A Child's Faith

"Jesus loves me, this I know,
For the BIBLE tells me so"
Little children ask no more,
For love is all they're looking for,
And in a small child's shining eyes
The FAITH of all the ages lies
And tiny hands and tousled heads
That kneel in prayer by little beds
Are closer to the dear Lord's heart
And of His Kingdom more a part
Than we who search, and never find,
The answers to our questioning mind
For faith in things we cannot see
Requires a child's simplicity
For, lost in life's complexities,
We drift upon uncharted seas
And slowly FAITH disintegrates
While wealth and power accumulates—
And the more man learns, the less he knows,

And the more involved his thinking grows
And, in his arrogance and pride,
No longer is man satisfied
To place his confidence and love
With childlike FAITH in God above—
Oh, Father, grant once more to men
A simple childlike FAITH again
And, with a small child's trusting eyes,
May all men come to realize
That FAITH alone can save man's soul
And lead him to a HIGHER GOAL.

God, Open My Eyes

God open my eyes
      so I may see
And feel Your presence
      close to me,
Give me strength
      for my stumbling feet
As I battle the crowd
      on life's busy street,
And widen the vision
      of my unseeing eyes
So in passing faces
      I'll recognize
Not just a stranger,
      unloved and unknown,
But a friend with a heart
      that is much like my own,
Give me perception
      to make me aware
That scattered profusely
      on life's thoroughfare
Are the best gifts of God
      that we daily pass by
As we look at the world
      with an UNSEEING EYE.

5

Poems for Troubled Times

Remember, God is ready and willing to help you. All you have to do is reach out your hand and you will find Him. He's only a prayer away.

—HSR

Let Go and Let God!

When you're troubled and worried and sick at heart
And your plans are upset and your world falls apart,
Remember God's ready and waiting to share
The burden you find much too heavy to bear—
So with faith LET GO AND LET GOD lead the way
Into a brighter and less troubled day.

Life Is a Mixture of Sunshine and Rain

Life is a mixture
    of sunshine and rain,
Laughter and teardrops,
    pleasure and pain—
Low tides and high tides,
    mountains and plains,
Triumphs, defeats
    and losses and gains—
But always in all ways
    God's guiding and leading
And He alone knows
    the things we're most needing—
And when He sends sorrow
    or some dreaded affliction,
Be assured that it comes
    with God's kind benediction—
And if we accept it
    as a gift of His love,
We'll be showered with blessings
    from OUR FATHER ABOVE.

Mrs. Rice was introduced to the Bible as a child and recalled sitting at the knees of both her mother and Grandmother Steiner, who read to her often from God's Word. One of her favorite passages was the Twenty-Third Psalm. "My advice," she wrote once to a troubled correspondent, "is to read that chapter when you first wake up. Read it very slowly and carefully and with deep meditation. Let your mind soak up the wonderful assurance in those words. It is the most powerful piece of writing in the world and it can heal any hurt the world inflicts."

There's Peace and Calm
in the 23rd Psalm

With THE LORD as "YOUR SHEPHERD"
    you have all that you need,
For, if you "FOLLOW IN HIS FOOTSTEPS"
    wherever HE may lead,
HE will guard and guide and keep you
    in HIS loving, watchful care
And, when traveling in "dark valleys,"
    "YOUR SHEPHERD" will be there...
HIS goodness is unfailing,
    HIS kindness knows no end,
For THE LORD is a "GOOD SHEPHERD"
    on whom you can depend...
So when your heart is troubled,
    you'll find quiet, peace and calm
If you open up the Bible
    and just read this treasured Psalm.

How to Build a Fortress of Faith

It's easy to say "in God we trust"
When life is radiant and fair,
But the test of faith is only found
When there are burdens to bear—
For our claim to faith in the "sunshine"
Is really no faith at all,
For when roads are smooth and days are bright
Our need for God is so small,
And no one discovers the fullness
Of the greatness of God's love
Unless they have walked in the "darkness"
With only a light from above—
For the faith to endure whatever comes
Is born of sorrow and trials,
And strengthened only by discipline
And nurtured by self-denials—
So be not disheartened by troubles,
For trials are the building blocks
On which to erect a fortress of faith
Secure on God's "ageless rocks."

The Message of the Fire Lily

The crackling flames rise skyward
    as the waving grass is burned,
But from the fire on the veld
    A great truth can be learned.
For the green and living hillside
    becomes a funeral pyre
As all the grass across the veld
    is swallowed by the fire.
What yesterday was living,
    today is dead and still,
But soon a breathless miracle
    takes place upon the hill.
For, from the blackened ruins
    there arises life anew
And scarlet lilies lift their heads
    where once the veld grass grew.
And so again the mystery
    of life and death is wrought,
And man can find assurance
    in this soul-inspiring thought,
That from a bed of ashes
    the fire lilies grew,
And from the ashes of our lives
    God resurrects us, too.

The Seasons of the Soul

Why am I cast down
    and despondently sad
When I long to be happy
    and joyous and glad?
Why is my heart heavy
    with unfathomable weight
As I try to escape
    this soul-saddened state?
I ask myself often
    "What makes life this way?
Why is the song silenced
    in the heart that was gay?"
And then with God's help
    it all becomes clear.

The soul has its seasons
     just the same as the year.
I too must pass through
     life's autumn of dying,
A desolate period
     of heart-hurt and crying,
Followed by winter
     in whose frostbitten hand
My heart is as frozen
     as the snow-covered land.
Yes, man too must pass
     through the seasons God sends,
Content in the knowledge
     that everything ends,

And oh what a blessing
        to know there are reasons
And to find that our soul
        must, too, have its seasons—
Bounteous seasons,
        and barren ones, too,
Times for rejoicing
        and times to be blue,
But meeting these seasons
        of dark desolation
With strength that is born
        of anticipation
That comes from knowing
        that "autumn-time sadness"
Will surely be followed
        by a "Springtime of Gladness."

Let Not Your Heart Be Troubled

Whenever I am troubled
    and lost in deep despair
I bundle all my troubles up
    and go to God in prayer.

I tell Him I am heartsick
    and lost and lonely, too,
That my mind is deeply burdened
    and I don't know what to do.

But I know He stilled the tempest
    and calmed the angry sea
And I humbly ask if in His love
    He'll do the same for me.

And then I just keep quiet
    and think only thoughts of peace
And if I abide in stillness
    my restless murmurings cease.

6

Poems that Bring Hope for Tomorrow

Tomorrow may hold your fate, tomorrow may mean your victory ...The great joy of expectation...the wonderment of an unknown realm...the splendor of the vast unlimited future lay in the eternal tomorrow.

—HSR

Trust Your Lord and Saviour

Take the Saviour's loving hand
 and do not try to understand,
Just let Him lead you where He will
 through pastures green, by waters still,
And place yourself in His loving care
 and He will gladly help you bear
Whatever lies ahead of you
 He will see you safely through,
No earthly pain is ever too much
 if God bestows His merciful touch.

God Sends Us Hope for Tomorrow

On the wings of death and sorrow
God sends us hope for tomorrow—
And in His mercy and His grace,
He gives us strength to bravely face,
The lonely days that stretch ahead
And know our loved one is not dead,
But only sleeping and out of sight
In that land where there is no night.

One thing never changes,
    It remains the same forever,
God truly loves His children
    And He will forsake them never.

For the Believer, Spring Is Eternal

All nature heeds the call of Spring
    as God awakens everything
And all that seemed so dead and still
    experiences a sudden thrill
As Springtime lays a magic hand
    across God's vast and fertile land—
Oh, how can anyone stand by
    and watch a sapphire Springtime sky
Or see a fragile flower break through
    what just a day ago or two
Seemed barren ground still hard with frost,
    but in God's world no life is lost,
And flowers sleep beneath the ground
    but when they hear Spring's waking sound
They push themselves through layers of clay
    to reach the sunlight of God's Day—
And man, like flowers, too, must sleep
    until he is called from the "darkened deep"
To live in that place where angels sing
    and where there is Eternal Spring!

Only the Love of God Endures

Everything in life is passing
    and whatever we possess
Cannot endure forever
    but ends in nothingness,
For there are no safety boxes
    nor vaults that can contain
The possessions we collected
    and desire to retain...
So all that man acquires,
    be it power, fame or jewels,
Is but limited and earthly,
    only "treasure made for fools"...

For only in God's Kingdom
    can man find enduring treasure,
Priceless gifts of love and beauty—
    more than mortal man can measure,
And the "riches" he accumulates,
    he can keep and part with never,
For only in God's Kingdom
    do our treasures last Forever…
So use the word "Forever"
    with sanctity and love,
For Nothing Is Forever
    But The Love of God Above!

A Stepping Stone to Life

When death brings weeping
And the heart is filled with sorrow,
It beckons us to seek God
As we ask about tomorrow...
And in these hours of "heart-hurt"
We draw closer to believing
That even death in God's Hands
Is not a cause for grieving
But a time for joy in knowing
Death is just a steppingstone
To a Life that's Everlasting
Such as we have never known.

The Way of the Cross Is the Way to God

He carried the cross to Calvary,
Carried its burden for you and me,
There on the cross He was crucified
And, because He suffered and bled and died,
We know that whatever our cross may be,
It leads to God and eternity.
For who can hope for a "crown of stars"
Unless it is earned with suffering and scars,
For how could we face the living Lord
And rightfully claim His promised reward
If we have not carried our cross of care
And tasted the cup of bitter despair.
Let those who yearn for the pleasures of life,
And long to escape all suffering and strife,
Rush recklessly on to an "empty goal"
With never a thought of the spirit and soul.
But if you are searching to find the way
To life everlasting and eternal day—
With Faith in your heart take the path He trod,
For the way of the cross is the way to God.

Spring Sings the Resurrection Glory

They asked me how I know it's true
That the Saviour lived and died
And if I believe the story
That the Lord was crucified?
And I have so many answers
To prove His Holy Being,
Answers that are everywhere
Within the realm of seeing:
The leaves that fell at autumn
And were buried in the sod
Now budding on the tree boughs
To lift their arms to God,
The flowers that were covered
And entombed beneath the snow
Pushing through the "darkness"
To bid the Spring "hello"
On every side Great Nature
Retells the Easter Story—
So who am I to question
The Resurrection Glory.

Albrecht Dürer, a renowned German Renaissance painter, is most famous for his work, "Praying Hands." The story behind the painting fascinated Mrs. Rice and she retold it in verse. Briefly, Dürer and a friend both wanted to devote their lives to painting, and both reportedly were inordinately gifted. But lack of money threatened their careers until Dürer's friend volunteered to take work as a manual laborer to support them.

Dürer protested that that was unfair, but his friend insisted, reasoning that later, when they could afford it, he would resume his lessons and his career. But the heavy work affected the young man's hands, so much so that he was unable to hold a brush. He never became a painter, but Dürer did, and one of his most lasting and most inspiring works is of his friend's sacrificial hands folded in prayer.

The Praying Hands

The *"Praying Hands"* are much, much more
    than just a work of art,
They are the "soul's creation"
    of a deeply thankful heart—
They are a *Priceless Masterpiece*
    that love alone could paint,
And they reveal the selflessness
    of an unheralded saint—
These hands so scarred and toilworn,
    tell the story of a man
Who sacrificed his talent
    in accordance with God's Plan—
For in God's Plan are many things
    man cannot understand,
But we must trust God's judgment
    and be guided by His Hand—
Sometimes He asks us to give up
    our dreams of happiness,
Sometimes we must forego our hopes
    of fortune and success —

Not all of us can triumph
    or rise to heights of fame,
And many times *What Should Be Ours,*
    goes to *Another Name*—
But he who makes a sacrifice,
    so another may succeed,
Is indeed a true disciple
    of our blessed Saviour's creed—
For when we "give ourselves away"
    in sacrifice and love,
We are "laying up rich treasures"
    in God's kingdom up above—
And hidden in gnarled, toilworn hands
    is the truest *Art of Living,*
Achieved alone by those who've learned
    the *"Victory of Giving"*—
For any sacrifice on earth,
    made in the dear Lord's name,
Assures the giver of a place
    In heaven's Hall of Fame.

God Is No Stranger

God is no stranger in a faraway place,
He's as close as the wind
    that blows cross my face,
It's true I can't see the wind as it blows,
    but I feel it around me and my heart surely knows
That God's mighty hand can be felt every minute,
    for there is nothing on earth that God isn't in it—
The sky and the stars, the waves and the sea,
    the dew on the grass, the leaves on a tree
Are constant reminders of God and His nearness
    proclaiming His presence with crystal-like clearness,
So how could I think God was far, far away
    when I feel Him beside me every hour of the day,
And I've plenty of reasons to know God's my friend
    and that His is one friendship that time cannot end.

For I am persuaded that neither death, nor life, nor angels, nor principalities, nor powers, nor things present, nor things to come, nor height, nor depth, nor any other creature, shall be able to separate us from the love of God, which is in Christ Jesus our Lord.
—Romans 8:38-39

The End of the Road
Is But a Bend in the Road

When we feel we have nothing left to give
     and we are sure that the "song has ended"
When our day seems over and the shadows fall
     and the darkness of night has descended,
Where can we go to find the strength
     to valiantly keep on trying,
Where can we find the hand that will dry
     the tears that the heart is crying—
There's but one place to go and that is to God
     and, dropping all pretense and pride,
We can pour out our problems without restraint
     and gain strength with Him at our side—

And together we stand at life's crossroads
     and view what we think is the end,
But God has a much bigger vision
     and He tells us it's ONLY A BEND—
For the road goes on and is smoother,
     and the "Pause in the song" is a "rest,"
And the part that's unsung and unfinished
     is the sweetest and richest and best—
So rest and relax and grow stronger,
     LET GO and LET GOD share your load,
Your work is not finished or ended,
     you've just come to a bend in the road.

Yesterday, Today and Tomorrow!

Yesterday's dead,
Tomorrow's unborn,
So there's nothing to fear
And nothing to mourn
For all that is past
And all that has been
Can never return
To be lived once again—
And what lies ahead
Or the things that will be
Are still in God's Hands
So it is not up to me
To live in the future
That is God's great unknown,
For the past and the present
God claims for His own,

So all I need do
Is to live for Today
And trust God to show me
The Truth and the Way—
For it's only the memory
Of things that have been
And expecting Tomorrow
To bring trouble again
That fills my Today,
Which God wants to bless,
With uncertain fears
And borrowed distress—
For all I need live for
Is this one little minute,
For life's Here and Now
And Eternity's in it.

The Legend of the Raindrop

The legend of the raindrop
    has a lesson for us all
As it trembled in the heavens
    questioning whether it should fall—
For the glistening raindrop argued
    to the genie in the sky,
"I am beautiful and lovely
    as I sparkle here on high,
And hanging here I will become
    part of the rainbow's hue
And I'll shimmer like a diamond
    for all the world to view."
But the genie told the raindrop,
    "Do not hesitate to go,
For you will be more beautiful
    if you fall to earth below,
For you will sink into the soil
    and be lost a while from sight,
But when you reappear on earth,
    you'll be looked on with delight;

For you will be the raindrop
		that quenched the thirsty ground
And helped the lovely flowers
		to blossom all around,
And in your resurrection
		you'll appear in queenly clothes
With the beauty of the lily
		and the fragrance of the rose;
Then, when you wilt and wither,
		you'll become part of the earth
And make the soil more fertile
		and give new flowers birth."
For there is nothing ever lost
		or eternally neglected,
For everything God ever made
		Is always resurrected;
So trust God's all-wise wisdom
		and doubt the Father never,
For in His heavenly kingdom
		There is nothing lost forever.

7

*Poems for
Routing
Worry*

If I do my best, God will do the rest.
—HSR

I Meet God in the Morning

"The earth is the Lord's and the fullness thereof
    It speaks of His greatness, it sings of His love,"
And each day at dawning I lift my heart high
    And raise up my eyes to the infinite sky, .
I watch the night vanish as a new day is born,
    And hear the birds sing on the wings of the morn,
I see the dew glisten in crystal-like splendor,
    While God with a touch that is gentle and tender
Softly wraps up the night and tucks it away,
    And hangs out the sun to herald a new day…
And so I give thanks and my heart kneels to pray,
    "God keep me and guide me and go with me today."

Remember, there's no cloud too dark
        for God's light to penetrate,
If we keep on believing
        and have faith enough to wait.

Never Borrow Sorrow

Deal only with the present,
Never step into tomorrow,
For God asks us just to trust Him
And to never borrow sorrow—
For the future is not ours to know
and it may never be,
So let us live and give our best
And give it lavishly—
For to meet tomorrow's troubles
Before they are even ours
Is to anticipate the Saviour
And to doubt His all-wise powers—
So let us be content to solve
Our problems one by one,
Asking nothing of tomorrow
Except Thy will be done.

Anywhere Is a Place of Prayer

I have prayed on my knees in the morning,
I have prayed as I walked along,
I have prayed in the silence and darkness
And I've prayed to the tune of a song—
I have prayed in the midst of triumph
And I've prayed when I suffered defeat,
I have prayed on the sands of the seashore
Where the waves of the ocean beat—
I have prayed in a velvet-hushed forest
Where the quietness calmed my fears,
I have prayed through suffering and heartache
When my eyes were blinded with tears—
I have prayed in churches and chapels,
Cathedrals and synagogues, too,
But often I've had the feeling
That my prayers were not getting through,

And I realized then that our Father
Is not really concerned where we pray
Or impressed by our manner of worship
Or the eloquent words that we say...
He is only concerned with our feelings,
And He looks deep into our heart
And hears the "cry of our soul's deep need"
That no words could ever impart...
So it isn't the prayer that's expressive
Or offered in some special spot,
It's the sincere plea of a sinner
And God can tell whether or not
We honestly seek His forgiveness
And earnestly mean what we say,
And then and then only He answers
The prayer that we fervently pray.

Where There Is Love

Where there is love
    the heart is light,
Where there is love
    the day is bright,
Where there is love
    there is a song
To help when things
    are going wrong,
Where there is love
    there is a smile,
To make all things
    seem more worthwhile,
Where there is love
    there's quiet peace,
A tranquil place
    where turmoils cease—
Love changes darkness
    into light
And makes the heart
    take "wingless flight"—
Oh, blest are they
    who walk in love,
They also walk
    with God above.

Count Your Many Blessings

There are always two sides,
    the Good and the Bad,
The Dark and the Light,
    the Sad and the Glad—
But in looking back over
    the Good and the Bad
We're aware of the number
    of Good Things we've had—
And in counting our blessings
    we find when we're through
We've no reason at all
    to complain or be blue—
So thank God for Good things
    He has already done,
And be grateful to Him
    for the battles you've won,

And know that the same God
  who helped you before
Is ready and willing
  to help you once more—
Then with faith in your heart
  reach out for God's Hand
And accept what He sends,
  though you can't understand—
For Our Father in heaven
  always knows what is best,
And if you trust in His wisdom
  your life will be blest,
For always remember
  that whate'er betide you,
You are never alone
  for God is beside you.

My Daily Prayer

Bless me, heavenly Father
    forgive my erring ways,
Grant me strength to serve Thee,
    put purpose in my days.
Give me understanding
    enough to make me kind
So I may judge all people
    with my heart and not my mind.
And teach me to be patient
    in everything I do,
Content to trust Your wisdom
    and to follow after You.
And help me when I falter
    and hear me when I pray
And receive me in Thy kingdom
    to dwell with Thee some day.

8

Poems of Prayerful Praise and Thanksgiving

When you ask God for a gift,
  be thankful if He sends,
Not diamonds, pearls or riches,
  but the love of real, true friends.

—HSR

A Simple Prayer of Thanksgiving

I come not to ask, to plead or implore You,
I just come to tell You how much I adore You,
For to kneel in Your Presence makes me feel blest
For I know that You know all my needs best...
And it fills me with joy just to linger with You
As my soul You replenish and my heart You renew,
For prayer is much more than just asking for things—
It's the peace and contentment that quietness brings...
So thank You again for Your mercy and love
And for making me heir to YOUR KINGDOM ABOVE!

Grant Us Wisdom

God, grant us grace to use
      all the hours of our days,
Not for our own selfish interests
      and our own willful ways,
But teach us to take time for praying
      and for listening to you,
So each day is spent wisely
      doing what you want us to do.

On life's busy thoroughfare
we all meet angels unaware,
But we are too busy to listen or hear,
too busy to sense that God is near.

Give Us Understanding

O, God, our help in ages past,
    our hope in years to be,
Look down upon us all tonight
    and make us more like Thee,
Give us understanding,
    enough to make us kind,
So we may judge all people
    with our heart and not our mind.

It's a Comfort to Know

O, God, what a comfort
    to know that You care,
And to know when I seek You
    You will always be there.

God Is the Answer

In this restless world of struggle
It is often hard to find
Answers to the questions
That disturb our peace of mind,
And our hearts are lost and lonely
As we search to find the key
To the meaning of all living
And to immortality...
But we'll never find the answers
In science, graphs and charts,
For the only real solution
Must be found within our hearts...
For the answer to all living,
God holds safely in his keeping,
And only when we know Him
Will we find what we are seeking...
And to know Him is to love Him,
And to love Him is to find
The answers to all questions
That fill every troubled mind.

My Cross Is Not too Heavy

My cross is not too heavy,
My road is not too rough,
Because God walks beside me,
To know this is enough.

The Way, the Truth and the Life

I am the Way
    so just follow Me,
Though the way be rough
    and you cannot see.

I am the Truth
    which all men seek,
So heed not false prophets
    nor the words that they speak.

I am the Life
    and I hold the key
That opens the door
    to Eternity.

Thank You, God, for Little Things

Thank You, God, for little things
    that often come our way—
The things we take for granted
    but don't mention when we pray—
The unexpected courtesy,
    the thoughtful, kindly deed—
A hand reached out to help us
    in the time of sudden need—
Oh, make us more aware, dear God,
    of little daily graces
That come to us with "sweet surprise"
    from never-dreamed-of places.

The Solution to Our Problems

Everyone has problems
    in this restless world of care,
Everyone grows weary
    with the "cross they have to bear,"
Everyone is troubled
    and their skies are overcast
As they try to face the future
    while dwelling on the past,
But the people with their problems
    only listen with one ear,
For people only listen
    to the things they want to hear
And they only hear the kind of things
    they are able to believe
And the answers that are God's to give
    they're not ready to receive,
So while the peoples' problems
    keep growing every day
And man vainly tries to solve them
    in his own self-willed way,
God seeks to help and watches,
    waiting always patiently
To help them solve their problems
    whatever they may be—
So may the people of all nations
    at last become aware
That God will solve their problems
    through FAITH and HOPE and PRAYER.

The Light of the World Is Jesus

O, Father, up in heaven,
    we have wandered far away
From Jesus Christ, Our Saviour,
    who rose on Easter Day,
And the promise of salvation
    that God gave us when Christ died
We have often vaguely questioned,
    even doubted and denied,
We've forgotten why You sent us
    Jesus Christ, Your only Son,
And in arrogance and ignorance
    it's our will not Thine be done,
O, shed Thy light upon us
    as Easter dawns this year
And may we feel the presence
    of the risen Saviour near,
And, God, in Thy great wisdom,
    lead us in the way that's right,
And may the darkness of the world
    be conquered by Thy light.

Make Every Day Thanksgiving

Thank you, God, for everything—
     the big things and the small,
For every good gift comes from God—
     the giver of them all,
Too often we accept
     without any thanks or praise
The gifts God sends as blessing
     each day in many ways,
O, make us more aware, dear God,
     of little daily graces
That come to us with sweet surprise
     from never-dreamed-of places,
And help us to remember
     that the key to life and living
Is to make each prayer a prayer of thanks
     and every day THANKSGIVING.

And in Closing...

If you found any beauty
 in the poems of this book
Or some peace and some comfort
 in a word or line,
Don't give me praise
 or worldly acclaim
For the words that you read
 are not mine...
I borrowed them all
 to share with you
From our HEAVENLY FATHER
 above,
And the joy that you felt
 was GOD speaking to you
As HE flooded your heart
 with HIS LOVE.

—Helen Steiner Rice